CLASSIC DESIGNS FOR WOODCARVING

Richard Adam Dabrowski

S Sterling Publishing Co., Inc.   New York

ACKNOWLEDGMENTS

I am indebted to Mr. Richard C. Dabrowski for the photograph of Adam Dabrowski's work and for the use of the Trojan horse on page 56. Also to Mr. Ronald R. Roszkiewicz for his comments and assistance with technical details, and to Mr. Walter C. Hadley for the use of the box (page 63) from his private collection.

Special thanks is extended to the curators of the Dumbarton Oaks Museum, Washington, D.C. for permission to use material from the Pre-Columbian collection.

The advice concerning signs has added a special dimension to this book, and I thank Mr. David Hassan and Mr. Chuck Dorr for their significant contribution.

Library of Congress Cataloging-in-Publication Data

Dabrowski, Richard Adam.
  Classic designs for woodcarving.

  Includes index.
  1. Wood-carving—Patterns. I. Title.
TT199.7.D29   1987   730′.022′2   86-30180
ISBN 0-8069-6426-X (pbk.)

3   5   7   9   10   8   6   4   2

Copyright © 1987 by Richard A. Dabrowski
Published by Sterling Publishing Co., Inc.
Two Park Avenue, New York, N.Y. 10016
The material in this book was originally published by
Woodcraft Supply Corp. under the titles, "Designs
for the Woodcarver" and "Advanced Designs for
the Woodcarver," © 1976 and 1979, respectively, by
Richard Adam Dabrowski
Distributed in Canada by Oak Tree Press Ltd.
% Canadian Manda Group, P.O. Box 920, Station U
Toronto, Ontario, Canada M8Z 5P9
Distributed in the United Kingdom by Blandford Press
Link House, West Street, Poole, Dorset BH15 1LL, England
Distributed in Australia by Capricorn Ltd.
P.O. Box 665, Lane Cove, NSW 2066
Manufactured in the United States of America
All rights reserved

CONTENTS

DEDICATION

Trained as a sculptor in marble and stone at the National Art School in Warsaw, Poland, where he was born in 1880, Adam Dabrowski became the most masterful wood carver in America. He had studied and trained in his work for fifteen years both in Poland and in Russia. He came to the new world in 1906 and by 1912 had established himself in his own studio where he was sought after by the leading architects of the day. He was a sculptor in wood rather than a wood carver and without rival in this country in the art of the Grinling Gibbons style of undercutting.

His appreciation of beauty and the ability to master his medium has resulted in a trail of sensitive, expressive, vigorous, and skillfully carved works which he produced wherever he went.

FOREWORD

Within the past few years there has been a marked growth of interest in woodcarving. This art which flourished from the seventeenth century practically died out in the third and fourth decades of this century, at least from a commercial point of view. Consequently there are but few professional carvers available to give instructions in this art. Further, due to the decline in commercial carving most tool manufacturers have gone out of business and the choice of suitable wood is ever growing smaller. The average carver is therefore on his own to learn the three basics of carving, namely: the technique of carving, the idiosyncracies of wood, and the creating of designs. Few have the ability to both design and carve.

The average person is primarily interested in learning how to carve, and with practice an adequate technique can be developed. Often, however, the finding of a design is frustrating. Students constantly ask what can I carve? Where do you find designs for carving? Given a design, most self taught carvers can turn out a satisfying project. They soon learn to change some designs, by accident or otherwise, to suit their taste and, with practice, many will eventually create their own. To most, however, the fun is in the carving and none should be denied the pleasure of accomplishment because one cannot draw. It is to these carvers that this book is presented. The designs can be carved as plaques in varying degrees of bas relief or even in the round and will prove of value to all carvers regardless of individual proficiency. It is hoped that the author, in the future, will be able to present other editions of this valuable book.

Alexander P. Aitken, M.D.

Dr. Aitken, a retired orthopedic surgeon, is in his own right a woodcarver of considerable skill. Since taking up the art as a hobby in 1936 he has created hundreds of carvings, and has for some years been teaching wood carving.

Recently his splendidly designed and carved book stand was given the Popular Award at the New England Woodcarvers Association show.

INTRODUCTION

This book is dedicated to the woodcarver who is searching for designs to carve. Perhaps the most difficult thing for the carver is the invention of original designs. This is true also for other crafts, and it should be noted at the outset that many of these designs are useful to those pursuing marquetry, wood engraving, silk screen, tile design, jig saw puzzles, even needle point, embroidery, and rug hooking.

Inspiration often comes from viewing the work of artists from various cultures and different periods of time. Many such works of art make good designs for carving in relief. Unfortunately however, it is often difficult to translate a photo of an inspiring work of art to a two dimensional drawing suitable for transfer to a flat surface because of violent foreshortening, an unattractive angle of view, or murky shadows which obscure important details.

The beauty and interest of a carving depends on the shadows cast by the prevailing light. Close attention to the study of a design and its resolution into lights and shadows will assure a pleasing and dramatic outcome. Therefore, to create a successful relief carving it is necessary to make a few decisions before starting, such as:

Where will the finished piece be displayed?

Outdoors? Facing East — West, which way? High up or at eye level? Should it look its best in the morning light, at midday, sundown?

Indoors? Will it face a window, can it be lighted from the side, which side? Will it be placed at table height, eye level, near the ceiling?

Why all the fuss? Well, if it will be viewed slightly above eye level, with the light coming from the upper left, then it should be carved with this in mind.

While working on the piece place the light source so as to properly illuminate your work. From time to time take the piece to its approximate final position, light it as it will be lighted and check to see if your work is saying what it should say.

Do the outlines stand out sharply? Do the shadows fall where they should? Are you achieving "color" by contrast of light and shadow — in some places very subtley, in others very strongly, as may be required?

If your work is to be placed out doors go out to that place at various times of the day and observe the angle of the sun, the amount of light or shade caused by buildings or trees, and other factors which might affect the lighting, the background, the location. Then go inside and think while you work. Stop occasionally and take the piece outside at the time of day when you want it to be most effective. Set it in place and look at it. Study the problems. By solving them you will enhance your appreciation and develop your skill as an artist.

We assume, of course, that one knows something about technique, for this is not a how-to-do-it book, but a go-do-it book. The skill and experience of each individual woodcarver will govern the outcome. Every carver can at least follow the outline, round the edges and shape the details to produce a low relief. There are those who will decide to handle the project as medium or high relief. They may glue up planks and blocks to give the necessary height to produce dramatic high relief carving. Some of these designs even lend themselves to work in the round. For this, careful planning, creation of additional views with paper and pencil, and great skill, time, and patience will be required.

The patterns in this collection were derived from the work of artists of the past. They have been completely redrawn with the woodcarver in mind, and are simple and straightforward, and ready for use. They have been selected with a view to interest, variety, style, and point of origin. Most contain sufficient detail to afford carvers a reasonable challenge and an opportunity to use most of their tools and all of their skill.

These head-on patterns of birds, animals, ships and other designs were drawn with strong,clean delineation to enable woodcarvers to trace, or to enlarge, by using the grid system supplied, directly on to flat stock; to pick up their tools and begin to carve.

THE SEARCH FOR KNOWLEDGE

Copying for the purpose of study and enlightenment is not to be scorned, nor should it be avoided, as so many amateurs wrongly think. It is an efficient way to broaden understanding and appreciation of the object being studied.

Let us hasten to say that honesty and integrity and even the law enters the situation when person "A" copies the work of person "B". One simply does not pass off the work of another as one's own. However to copy a portion of a difficult subject to help develop a technique, to study the pattern of successive steps required to develop a design; even to copy the whole thing, and to give full credit to the originator and label one's own effort as a copy is necessary, acceptable and usual.

To the serious, determined carver the study/copy of designs, be they contemporary or ancient, traditional or modern, can be the stepping stone to originality, ingenuity, and creativity.

Then, by means of drawings, layouts, or even modeling prototypes in clay, development of one's ideas evolve, and the creation of the work at hand becomes one's own and original solution.

TRANSFERRING

WORK IN RELIEF

For reproducing or enlarging the use of a pantograph is the quickest, most direct manual method. Based on my own experience, a well built, accurately calibrated metal pantograph is well worth the investment.

Another customary and useful method is to square off the drawing, or, to preserve the original source, a copy or tracing of the drawing. Adding diagonals to the squares where needed to project more reference points assures more accuracy.

Also, if professional photography is available, a photographic enlargement directly to the required size is most satisfactory, but can be expensive. A small clay modelling of a detail will often clarify the design to the carver as no other system can.

WORK IN THE ROUND

Except for rudimentary forms, blocky or geometric, it is often easier to visualize the final design by making a small prototype. Clay, soap, or a block of cast plaster of Paris might be used to carve a model. If the transfer is to a block of the same size as the model, usually the significant points can be located with dividers. However, if the finished work is to be larger than the model a plumb line, level, and accurate proportional dividers are a necessity. Sometimes a skeleton frame work encompassing the cube is erected. A small one over the model and another to fit over the work to aid in sighting vertical and horizontal measurements, and to locate significant points.

PROPORTIONAL ENLARGEMENT/REDUCTION

The problem usually centers around the conversion of the length of a significant dimension to a new size or the relocation of reference points. After this key is established the layout and transferring can proceed.

A good method is described below, and we use as an example the problem to be solved in the newel post project (pages 78 and 79). When the turning is complete measure the circumference to be carved. Then —

1. Draw a line A-B, representing exactly the length to be altered. Mark off all significant points.

2. From either end of A-B, and at an angle to it, draw A-C exactly equal to the new length required.

3. Connect point B with point C.

4. Draw lines parallel to B-C, starting with each significant reference point on line A-B and ending by intersecting line A-C. Each point thus projected will be in a position which is in correct proportion to the original.

5. Using a compass, for the newel post project, scribe the new proportionally enlarged pattern from these projections.

Proportional Conversion

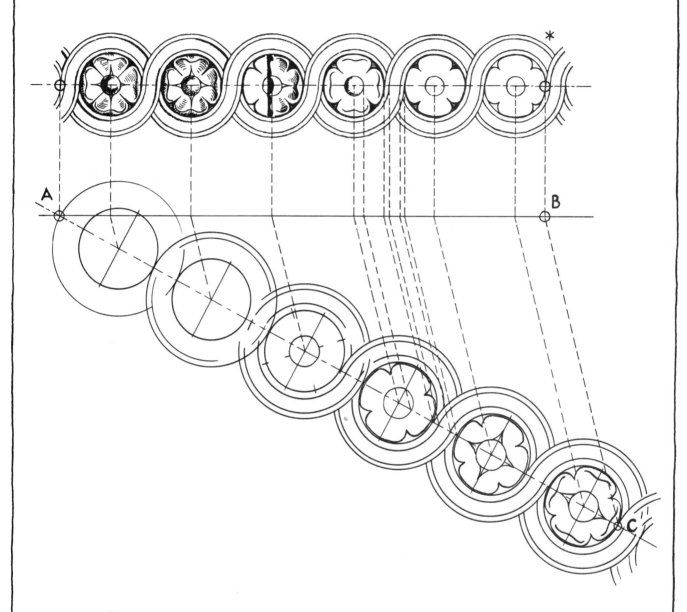

This procedure may be used either for enlargement or reduction

CORNUCOPIA   CIRCA 1880   PENNSYLVANIA

BALL PLAYERS   10TH CENTURY   MAYA

TEMPLE DOG   CIRCA 1830   CHINA

14

DOLPHINS   CIRCA 1802   NEW YORK

DOLPHIN   1840   LONDON

16

DRAGON   15TH CENTURY   CHINA

E PLURIBUS UNUM

GREAT SEAL OF THE UNITED STATES

146

COLLINS

EAGLE   20TH CENTURY   DELAWARE

EAGLE   CIRCA 1860   NEW YORK

EAGLE   CIRCA 1800   VERMONT

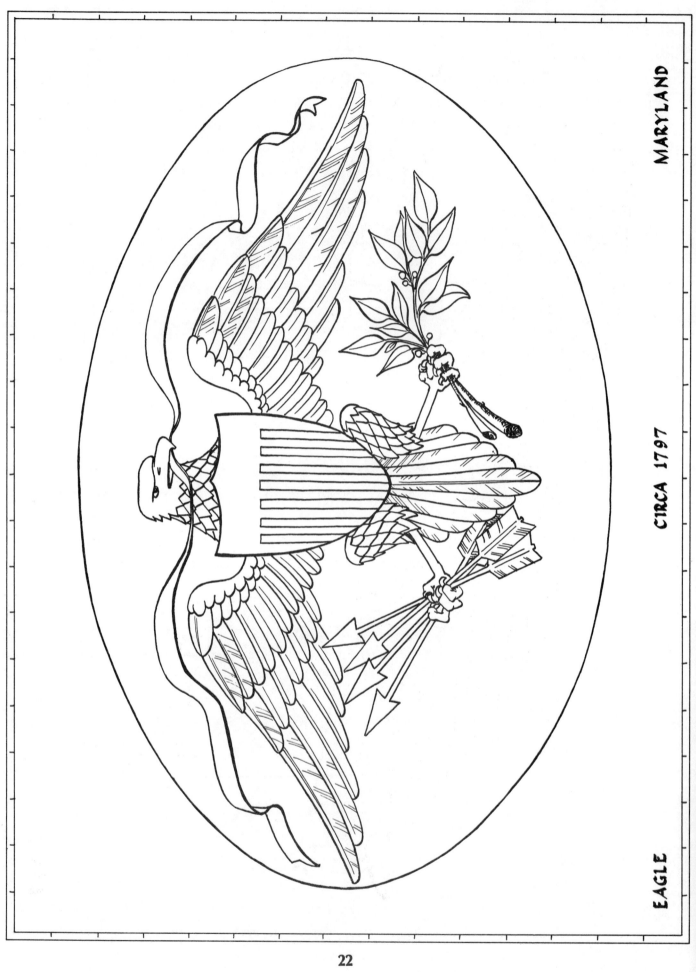

EAGLE CIRCA 1797 MARYLAND

22

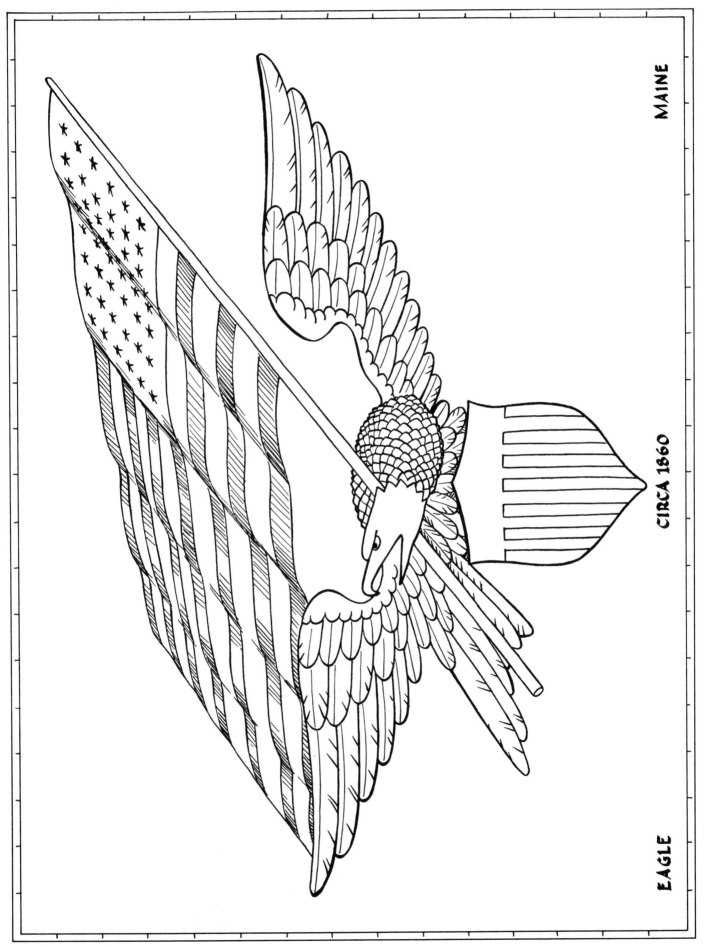

EAGLE

CIRCA 1860

MAINE

23

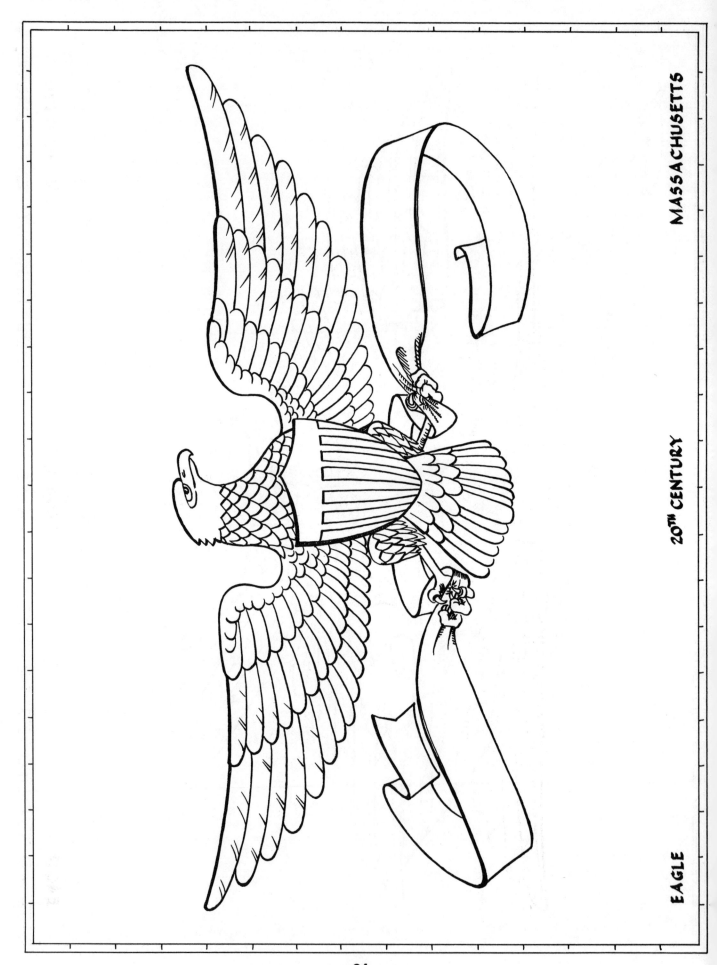

MASSACHUSETTS

20TH CENTURY

EAGLE

24

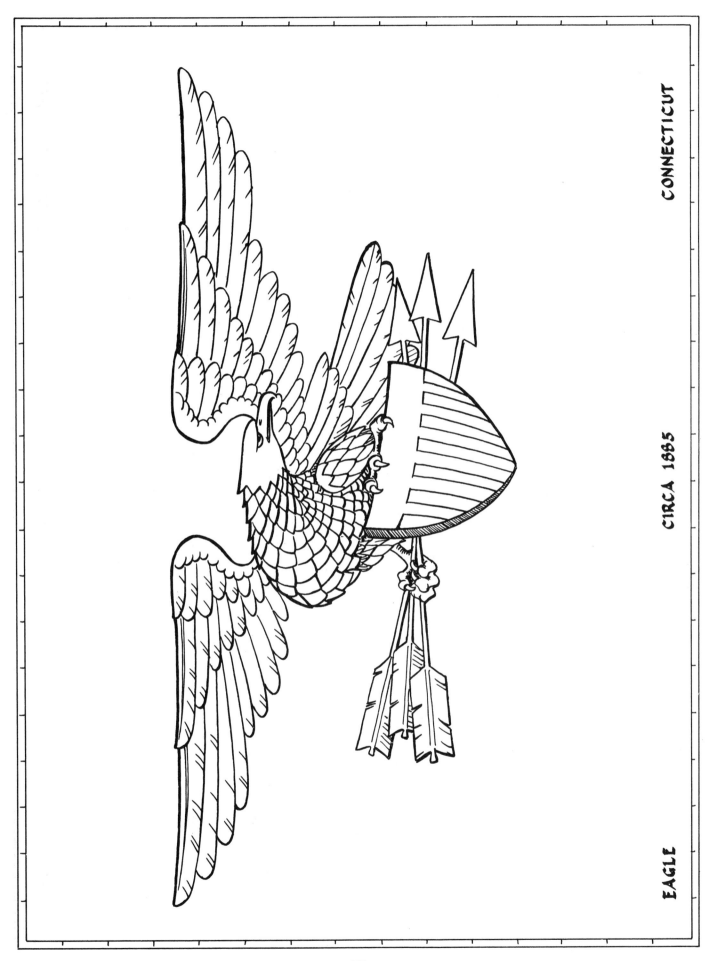

CIRCA 1885

EAGLE

25

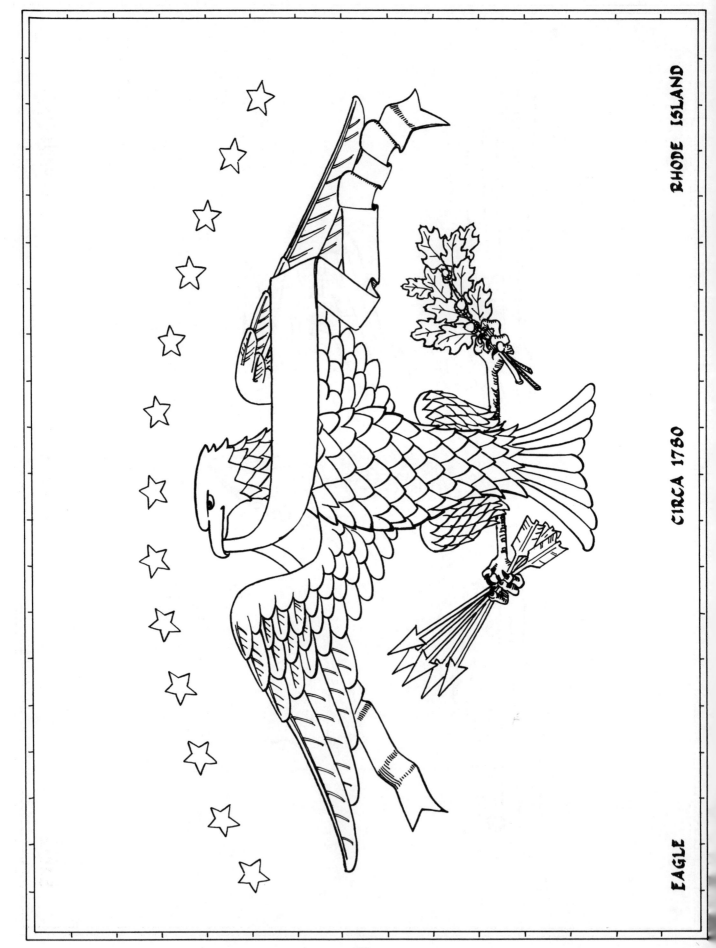

RHODE ISLAND

CIRCA 1780

EAGLE

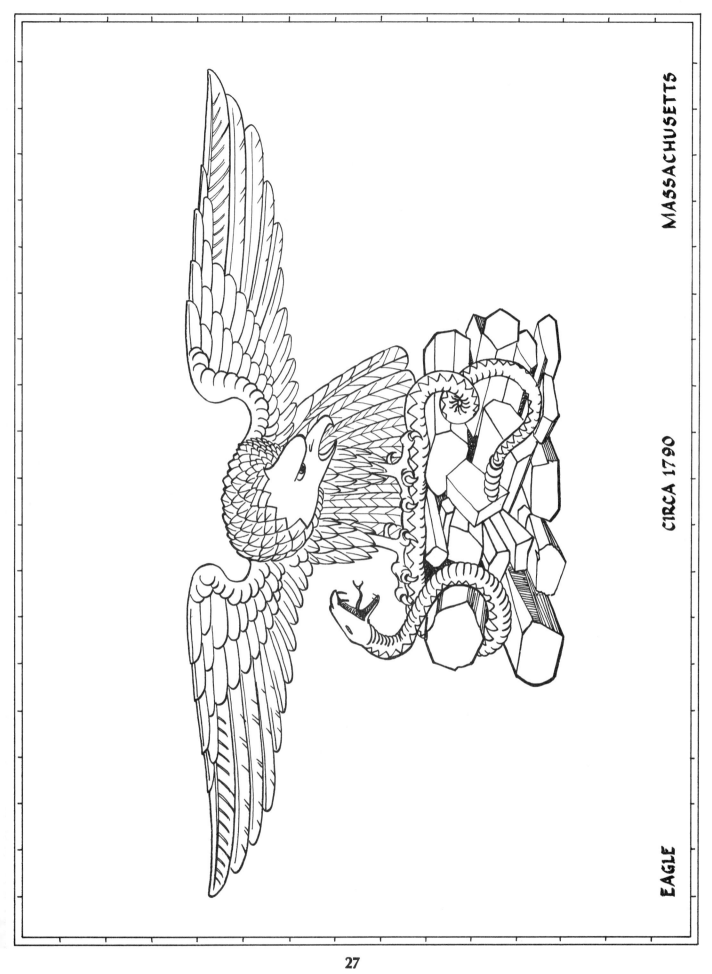

MASSACHUSETTS

CIRCA 1790

EAGLE

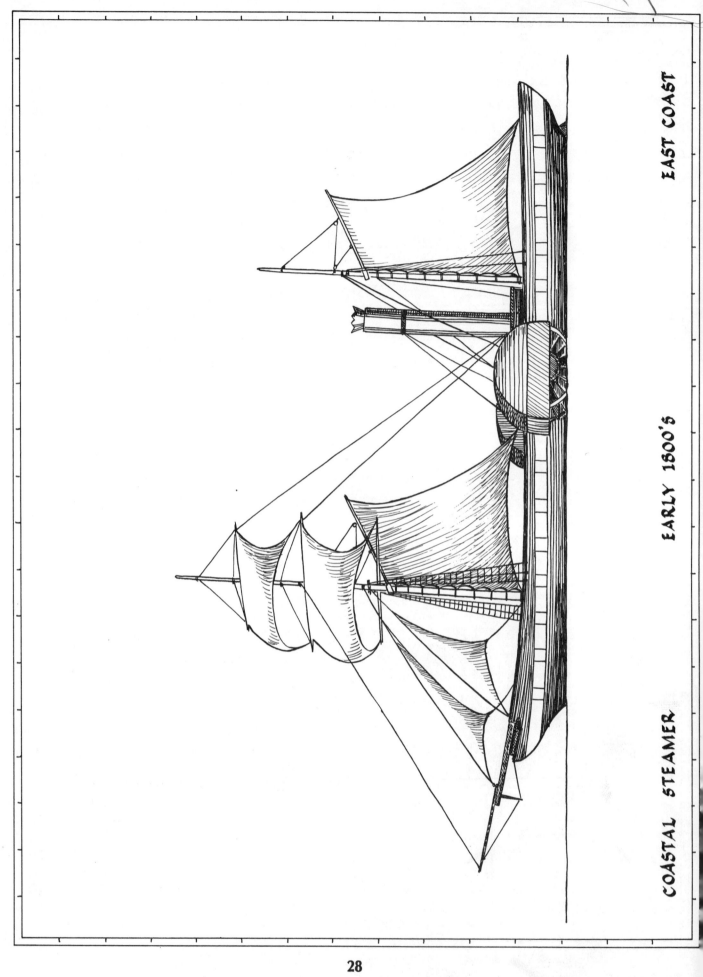

COASTAL STEAMER   EARLY 1800'S   EAST COAST

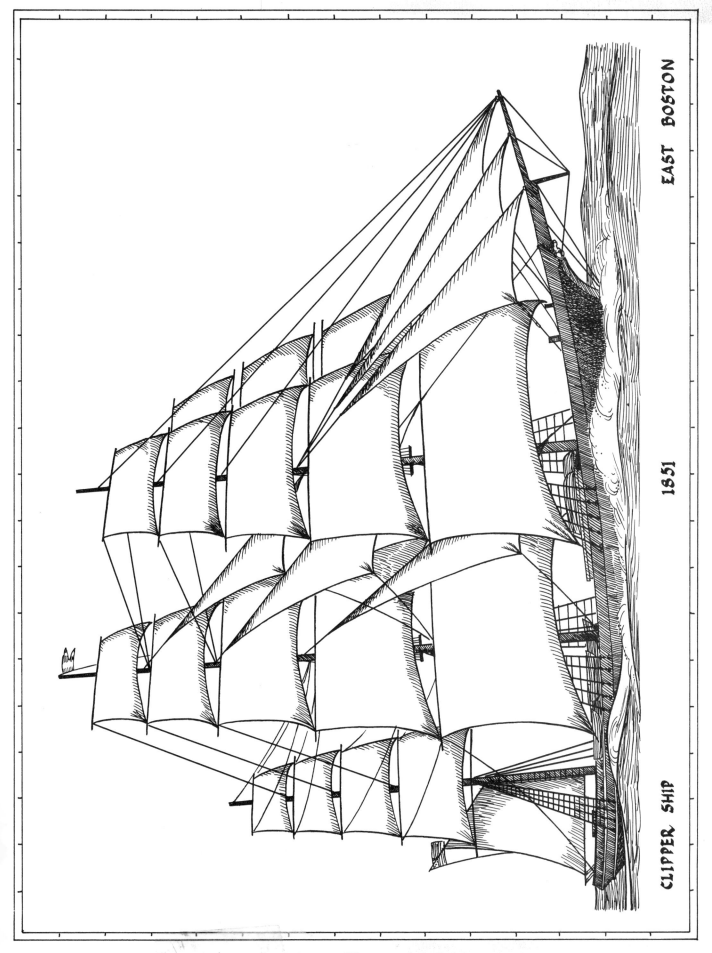

CLIPPER SHIP   1851   EAST BOSTON

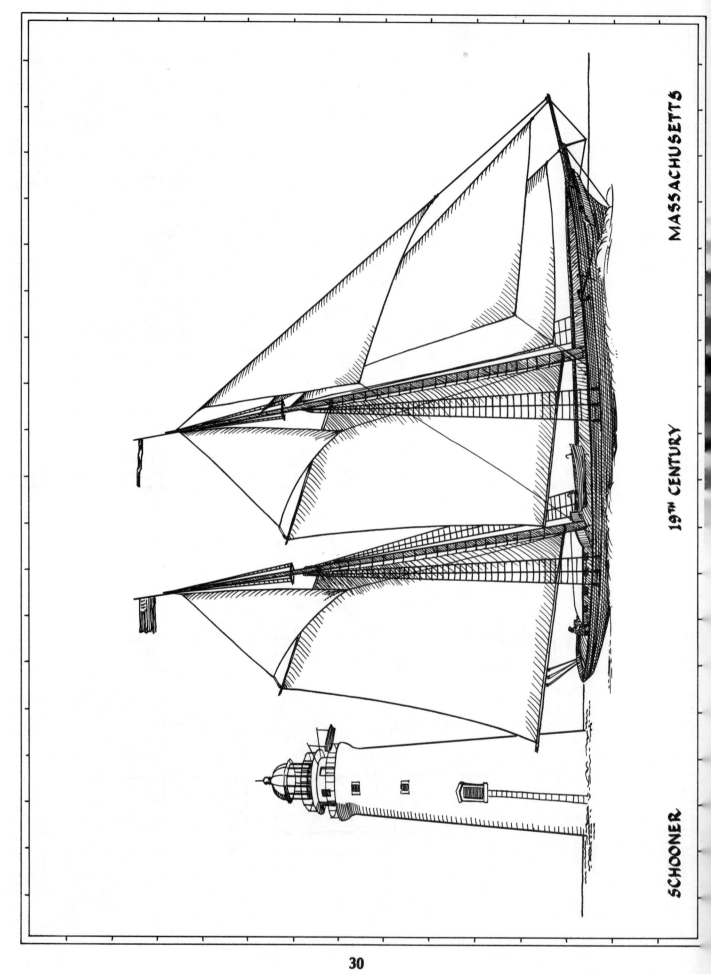

SCHOONER   19TH CENTURY   MASSACHUSETTS

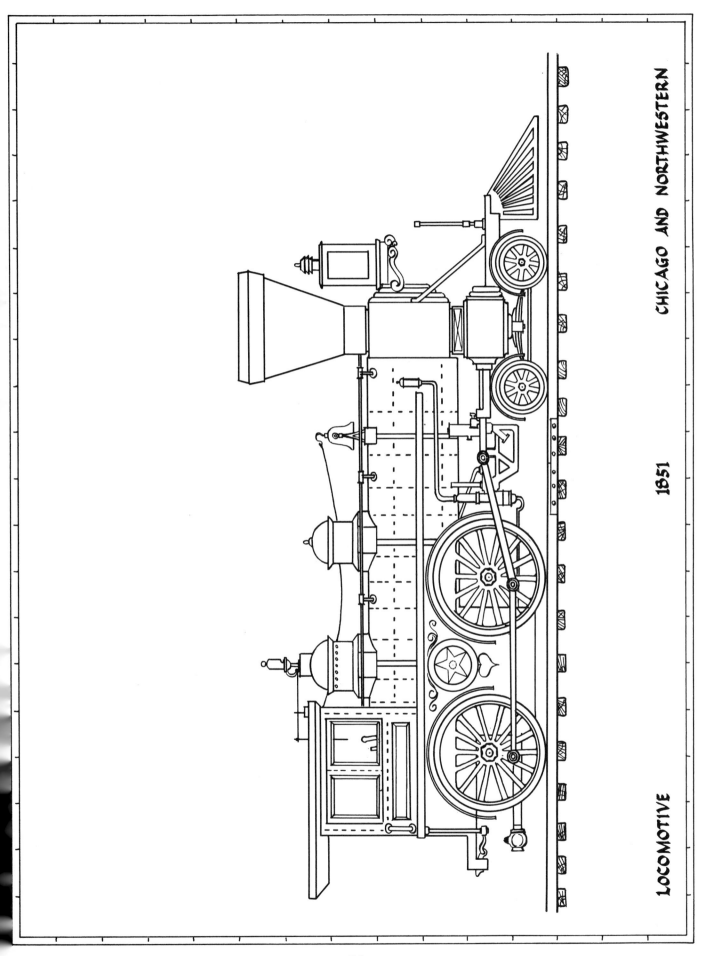

LOCOMOTIVE

1851

CHICAGO AND NORTHWESTERN

GARDEN SCENE · · · 19TH CENTURY · · · CHINA

FALCON   19TH CENTURY   CHINA

HEAD   8ᵀᴴ CENTURY   AZTEC

HEAD   4ᵀᴴ CENTURY   CELTIC

HEAD   16TH CENTURY   JAPAN

HEAD   11TH CENTURY   CHINA

HEAD   15TH CENTURY   BENIN

38

UNICORN   1870   LONDON

PEGASUS

20ᵀᴴ CENTURY

NEW YORK

PEGASUS   19TH CENTURY   NEW YORK

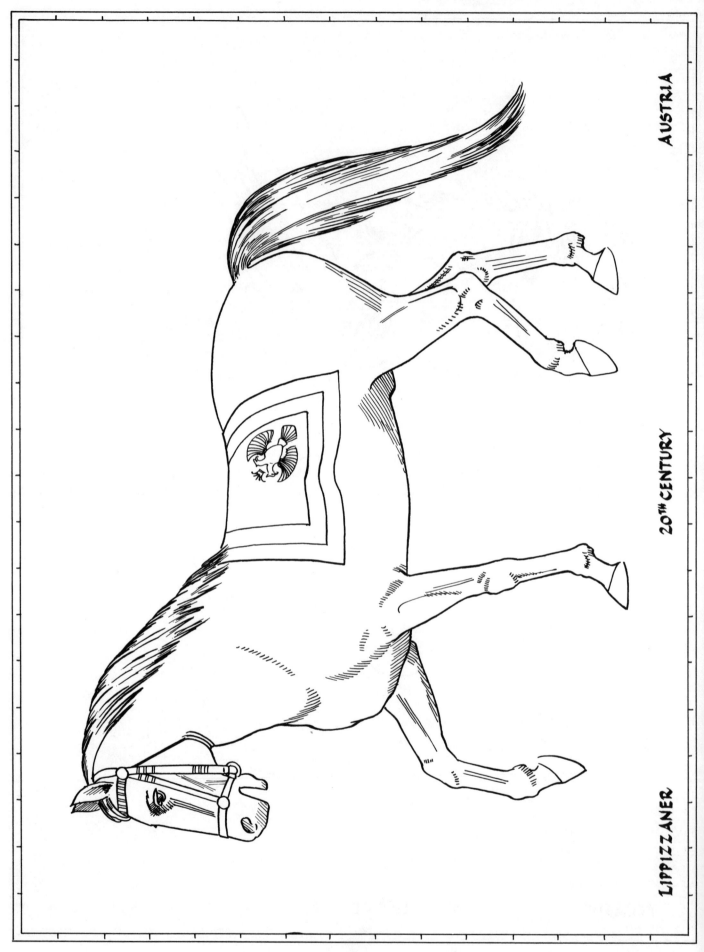

20TH CENTURY

LIPPIZZANER

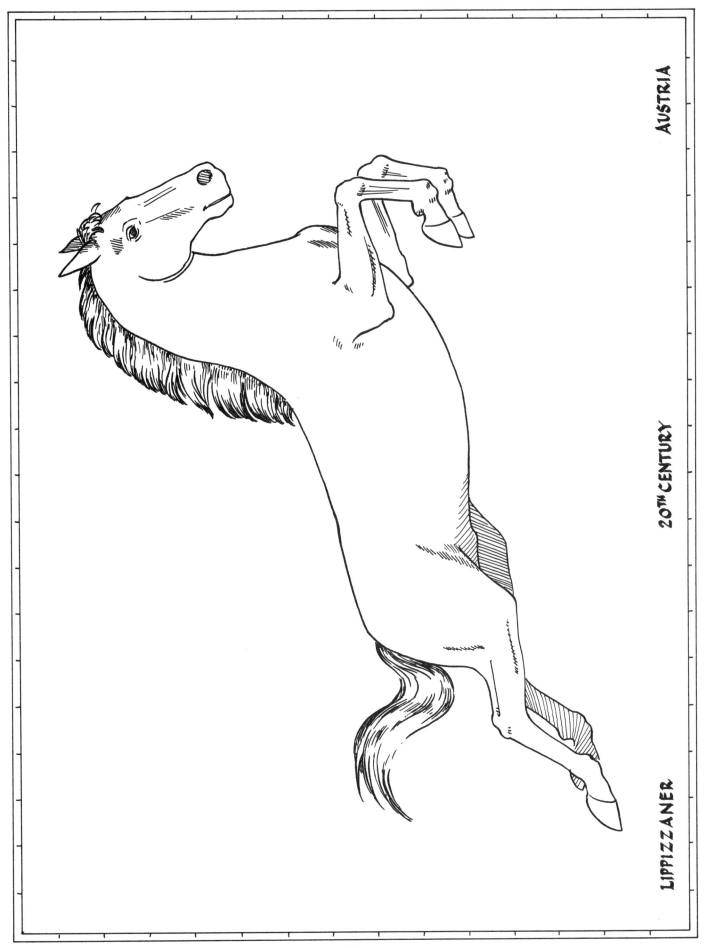

AUSTRIA

20TH CENTURY

LIPPIZZANER

43

MASK   13ᵀᴴ CENTURY   MAORI

44

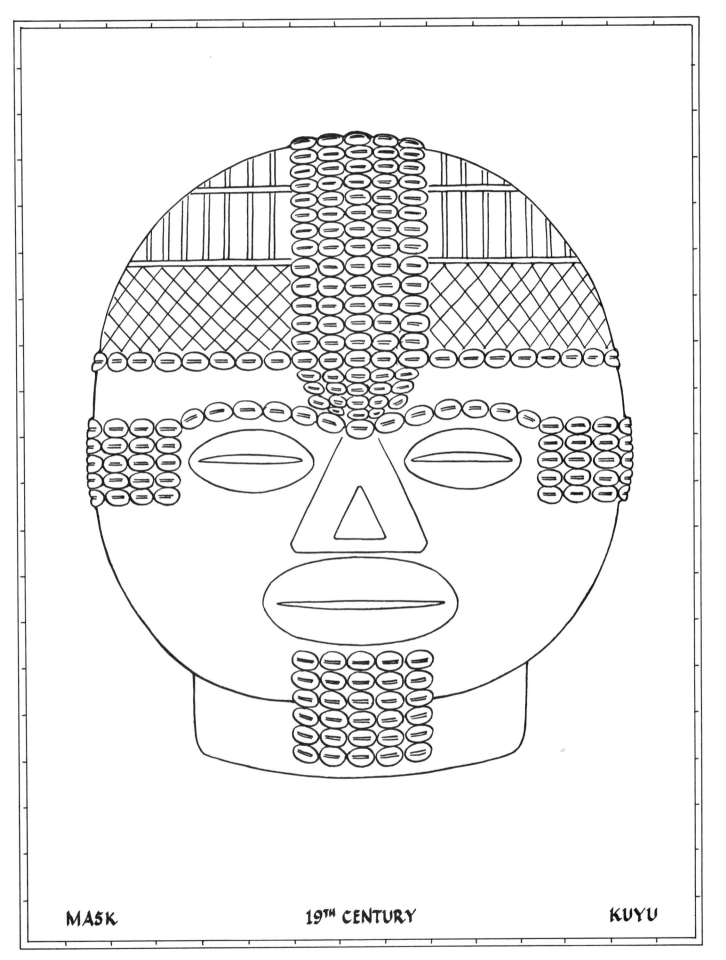

MA5K   19ᵀᴴ CENTURY   KUYU

45

BUDDHA AMIDA　　　　7ᵀᴴ CENTURY　　　　JAPAN

ROOSTER   20TH CENTURY   POLAND

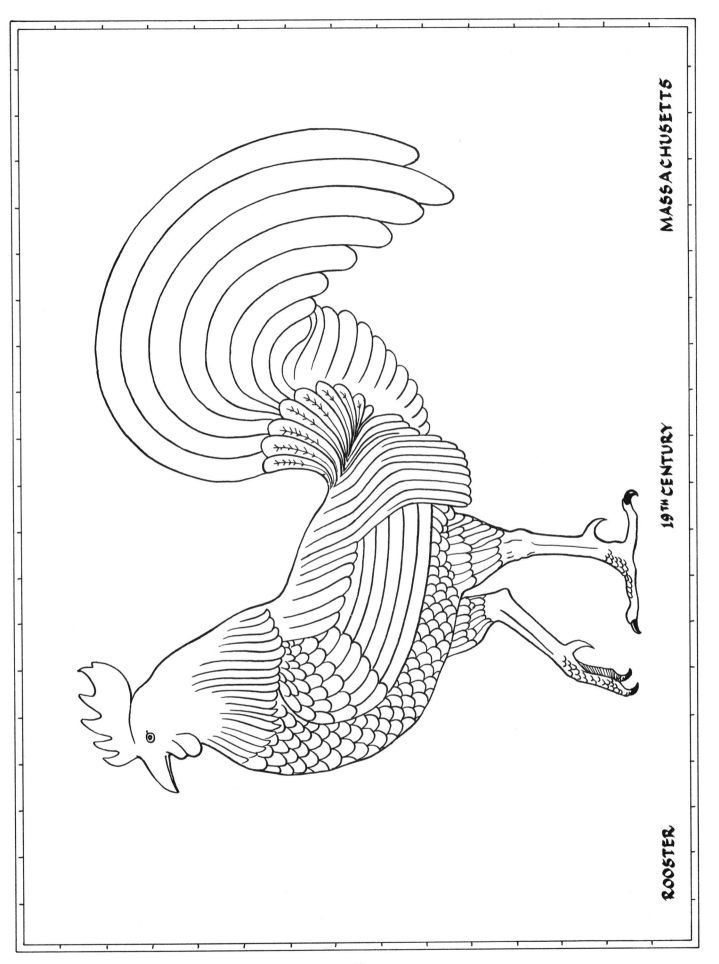

ROOSTER

19TH CENTURY

MASSACHUSETTS

OWL   CONTEMPORARY   NORTH AMERICA

OWL   4TH CENTURY   GREECE

SEA HORSE   CONTEMPORARY   ATLANTIC OCEAN

VIRGIN AND CHILD   14ᵀᴴ CENTURY   FLORENCE

ANGEL   13ᵀᴴ CENTURY   FLORENCE

Trojan Horse

Adam Dabrowski design   1948

This toy Trojan Horse will delight the imaginative
child. The finished size may be scaled to suit the
carver, but the original is about 1½" thick, 5¼" high
on its wheels, and made of clear pine. We suggest a
peanut oil finish because a small child may be tempted
to place the toy in its mouth. The wheels which are
assembled on dowels are securely cemented, for the
same reason.

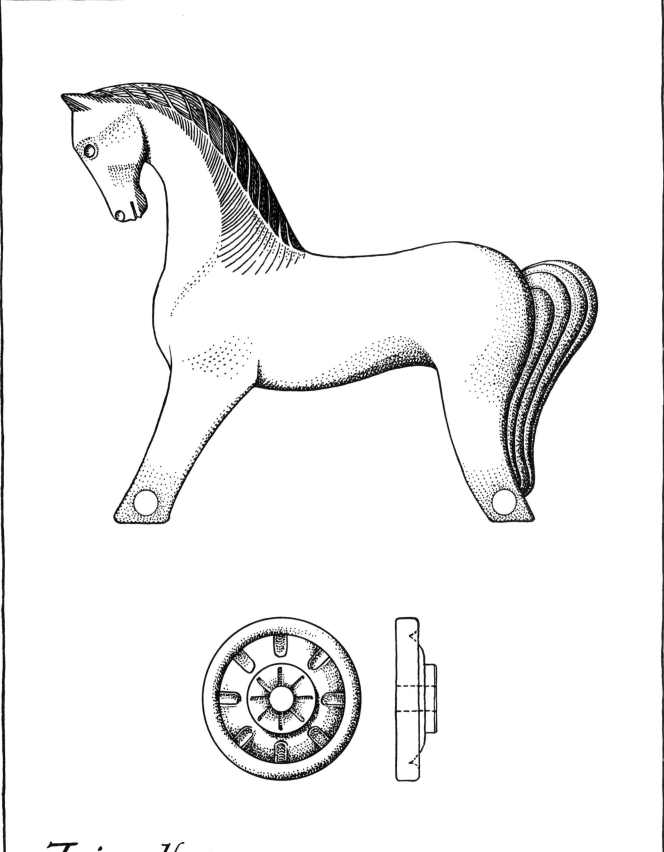

Trojan Horse

Mexico 300 A.D.

Carved Head   Mexico 300 A.D.
Dumbarton Oaks collection - Washington, D.C.

Black walnut is suggested. Head, 6″ x 12″ x 2″ thick. Base, 6″ x 6″ x 2″ thick. Use a pantograph to fit the drawing to the wood. Taper slightly the rectangular key at the bottom of the neck to fit the tapered slot in the base.

The design is essentially a two-sided high relief. Many such heads were found at Mexican temple sites. The originals are usually of polished stone. A smooth finish, and flowing lines and forms are the keynotes to this style of carving.

Decorate the edge of the base with a simple repeat-groove or herringbone pattern as shown below.

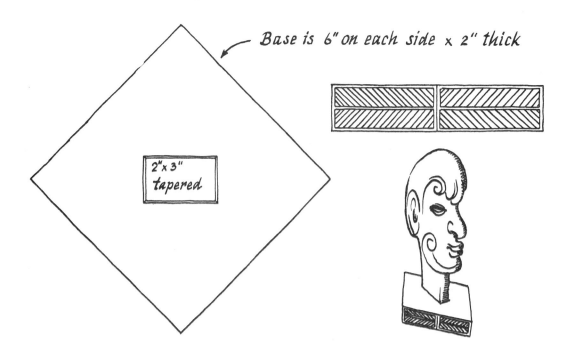

Base is 6″ on each side x 2″ thick

2″ x 3″ tapered

Trotter
From an Early American weather vane

This design may be treated as a relief carving on a plaque, or made into a sign, with or without the driver. In addition, the other side is shown for those who would like to make a three dimensional project of it. It is suggested, in this case, that the driver be carved separately and mounted on a scale model of the sulky made of flat metal and wire.

Old time moulds for hammering copper weather vanes were made of wood or cast metal. This horse pattern may be used for such a project.

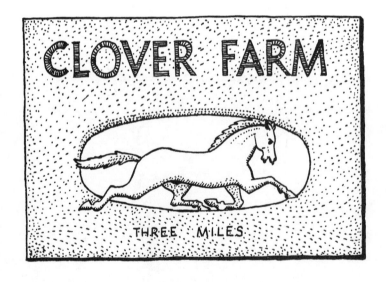

Other suggested applications

Trotter

Small Box

Adam Dabrowski design   circa 1947

The box is carved from a solid block of clear pine. Finished size: box, 4″ x 8¾″ x 1½″ thick; top, 4″ x 8¾″ x ⅞″ thick.

Note that the slight flair of the sides is carried up toward the top. This makes it easier to grasp when uncovering the box. The original is finished with a medium walnut stain, and wax.

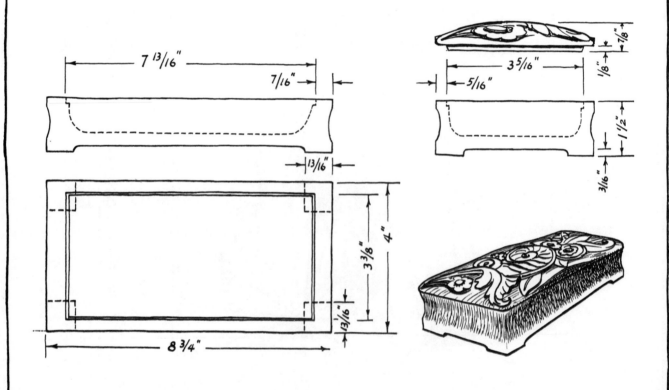

Small Box

Canisters

Contemporary adaptation

All the canisters are square. They may be fabricated of oak, walnut, or mahogany but not glued up until the carving has been completed. The following are the suggested dimensions:

large   9¼" high* x 6¼" square. Finial, 1¾" high x 1¹⁄₁₆" diameter

medium   7½" high* x 5⅛" square. Finial, 1½" high x ¹⁵⁄₁₆" diameter

small   5⅛" high* x 4¼" square. Finial, 1¹⁵⁄₁₆" high x ¹³⁄₁₆" diameter

*The height of each includes the top. The top for the large canister is 1" thick, the others may be proportionally a little thinner, if desired. The feet are 1" square x ¼" high.

With the above dimensions the relief designs for the front of each canister are proportioned to fit. Simply scale them up to the appropriate size. The berry and sausage pattern is suggested for the border of each carved panel.

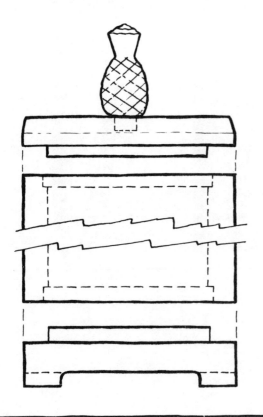

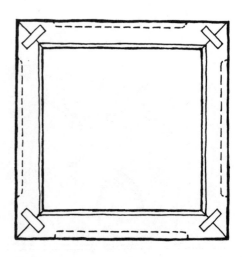

Construction Suggestions

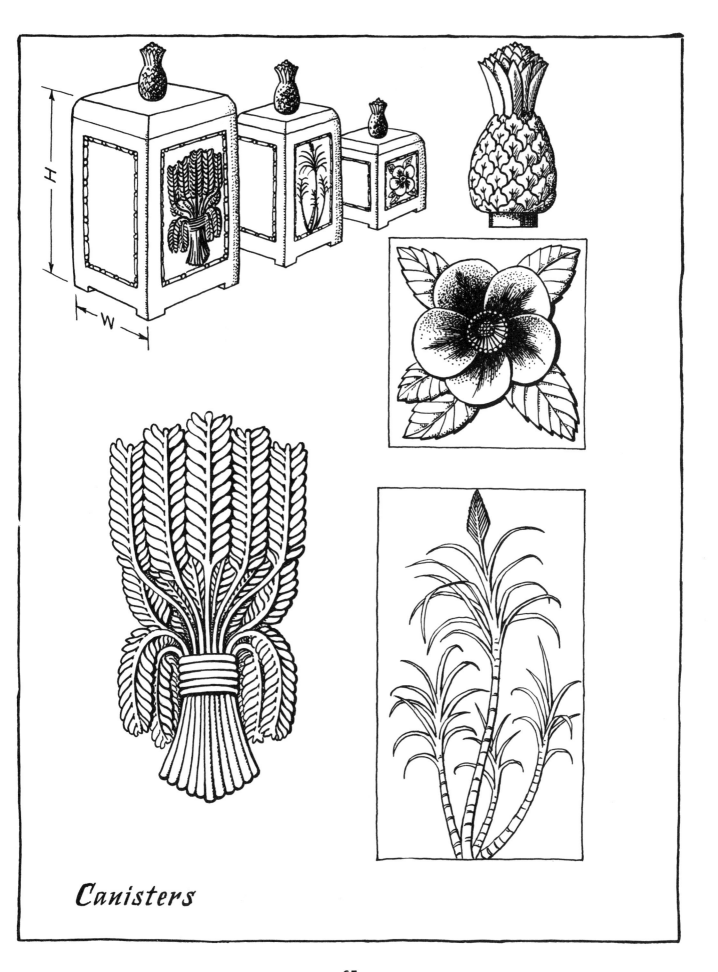

Canisters

Bellows

Designs adapted from the old and not so old

These simple wind machines can be a useful addition to almost any fire place. Suggested proportions are: for width, about 9½″ to 10½″, and for the overall height about 1.7 x (times) the width.

Fine examples of antique bellows exist. In the Renaissance period lavish ornamentation consisting of dolphins, masks, shells, birds, cherubs, griffins, dragons, and similar grotesque forms were notable features.

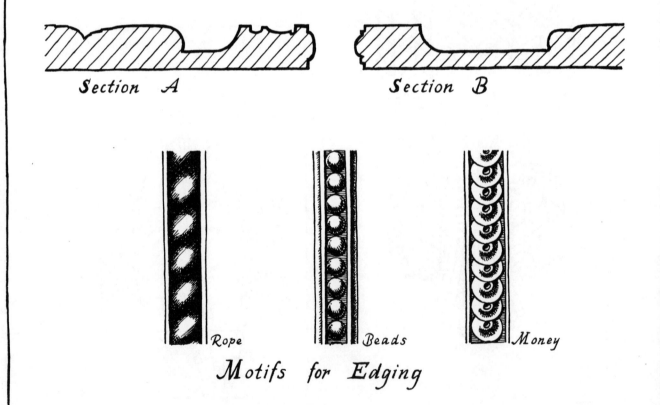

Section   A   Section   B

Rope   Beads   Money

Motifs   for   Edging

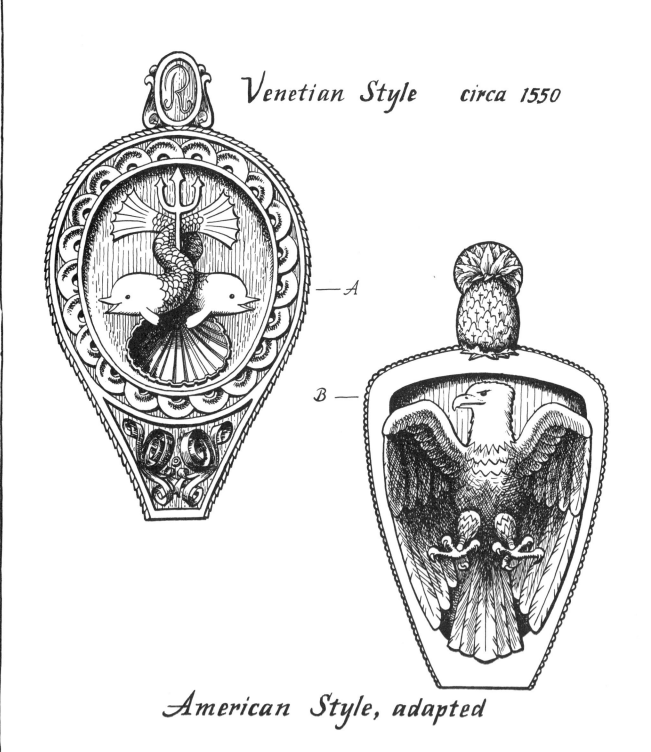

Venetian Style   circa 1550

— A

B —

American Style, adapted

Frame, Mahogany and Gold
Georgian design
Circa 1750

The frame is mahogany, 14¼" x 20¼" x ¾" thick, finished size. The crest is made of a separate block of mahogany, lime, or yellow pine, 11" x 4½" x 1¼" thick.

Draw the Acanthus leaf design, which is in Grinling Gibbons style, full size, on paper. Produce a natural flow of lines. Fret out the outline and cut the base of the crest to fit the frame. Do not smooth the surface of the carving. Tool marks give character to this style of work.

Lay out the conventional leaf work pattern on the glued up frame. Take care to space the pattern so that it comes out evenly at the corners. The berry and sausage motif will work well for the inner border. Trial and error layout with dividers gives the quickest solution for enclosed mouldings.

The gold leaf should be applied only to the crest and the carved portions of the frame.

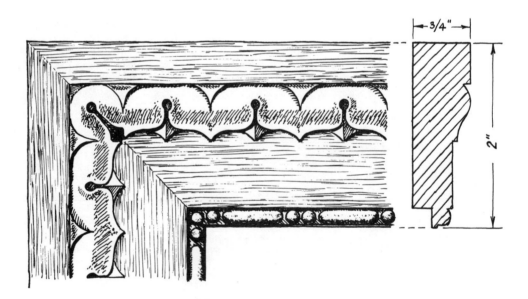

Frame, Mahogany and Gold

Dressing Table Mirror

Adam Dabrowski design   in Louis XIV style

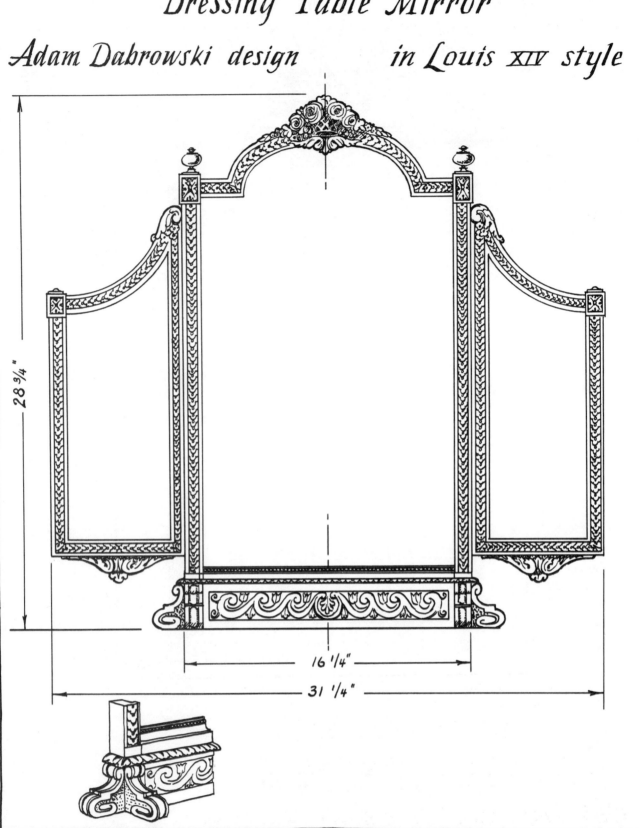

28 3/4 "

16 1/4 "

31 1/4 "

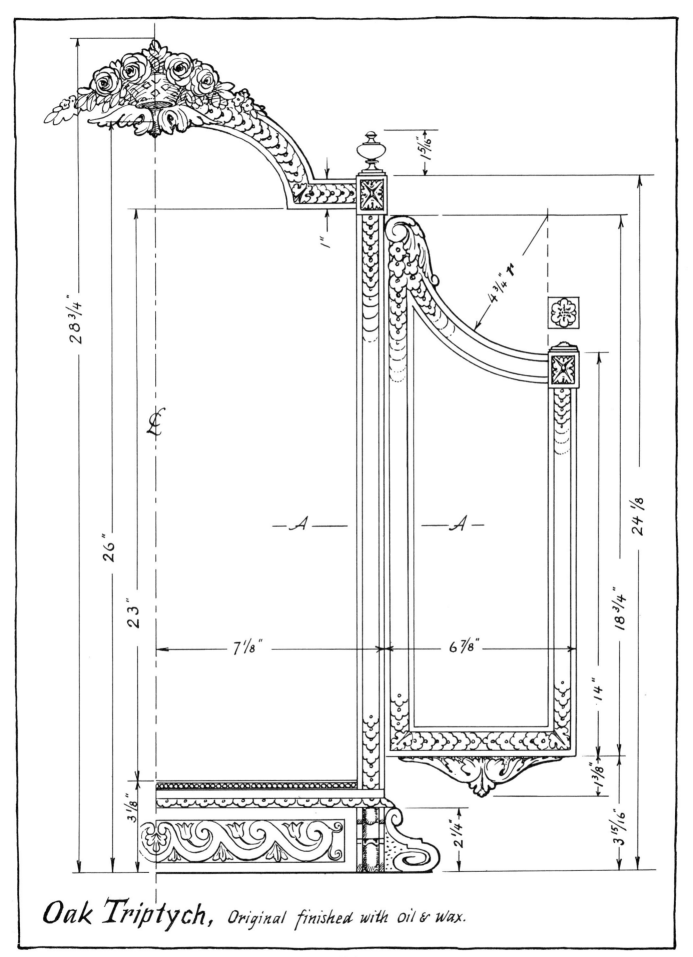

Oak Triptych, *Original finished with Oil & Wax.*

Details, dressing table mirror

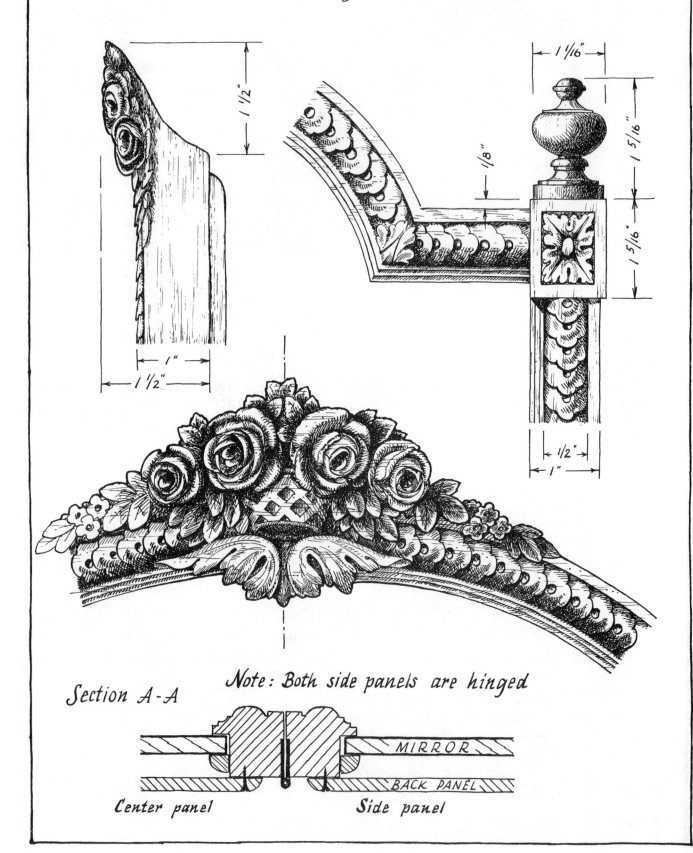

1 1/2"

1"

1 1/2"

1 1/16"

1/8"

1 5/16"

1 5/16"

1/2"

1"

Section A-A

Note: Both side panels are hinged

MIRROR

BACK PANEL

Center panel

Side panel

The original was carved of sugar pine, an unusual choice for such a detailed piece, involving extensive undercutting, and it demonstrates superb control over the material. Of course any fine grain wood such as pear, lime, or basswood will also produce satisfactory results in the hands of a true craftsman.

Wall panel, after Grinling Gibbons　　*Adam Dabrowski*

Sugar pine   24" x 30" x 4"　　　　　　　　　*1967*

Frame, Art Nouveau

Adam Dabrowski   New York - 1926

Use fine grain stock such as basswood. Finished size to be
8″ x 10″ x at least ¾″ thick. Cut the outline and the opening with a coping saw. The correct section-shape must be
carved directly into the wood. Cross sectional drawings,
below, show the variations due to the flow of the vine.

The original is finished with several of coats of wax and
then rubbed down. For best effect do not sandpaper; the
tool marks should remain visible.

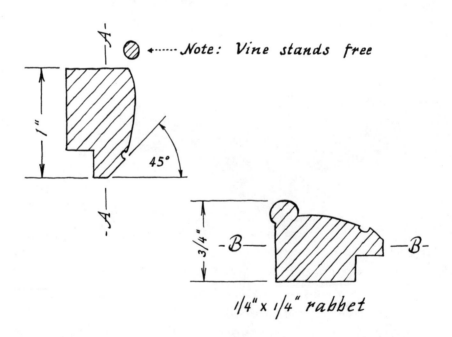

Note: Vine stands free

1″

45°

¾″

1/4″ x 1/4″ rabbet

Frame, Art Nouveau

Sgabello-Type Chairs
Side Chairs, Originated during Renaissance

Sgabello is the Italian word for a three-legged stool. Sgabello chairs were developed from these primitive stools by adding a back rest. The style is found in provincial work of all European countries. Usually the back board is very elaborate, with scroll cuts, often with pierced and carved panels.

They were made for earth or tile floors, and are ideally suited for modern patios, decks, and rustic kitchens. The Windsor chair has some similarity of construction.

Stock may be any stable, hard wood, such as maple, walnut, ash, or oak. Allow not less than 1½″ thickness for seats, and not less than 1″ for backs. The original chairs were often finished with wax alone.

CARPATHIAN MOUNTAIN STYLE
Adam Dabrowski   Circa 1920

SWISS   17th CENTURY
Metropolitan Museum of Art

Sgabello-Type Chairs

Turned and Carved Newel
Typical of sixteenth-century Flemish work

The newel post is turned from a block of cherry 6" x 6" x 18". Leave enough material for carving the cap of the acorn and the floral motif of the guilloche (gi losh). Guilloche patterns have been used throughout the ages. Assyrian, Greek, Roman, and Rennaisance craftsmen included them frequently in their work. All six elements of the interlaced bands are laid out in detail on page 11 for your reference because it is quite difficult to fit this pattern, with dividers only, to a predetermined length, such as the turned newel post.

After turning, measure the circumference produced, and on paper lay out the six elements using the drawing and the size conversion technique illustrated on page 11 to obtain the correct proportions.

All the small petal-like elements of the acorn are more or less the same size. The result is a curious irregularity in the ascending courses which tends to add interest to the form, and is somewhat similar to a real acorn cap. The very top row is set back a little, producing the chracteristic double row effect, with its delicate tooth pattern.

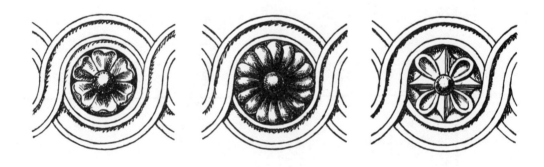

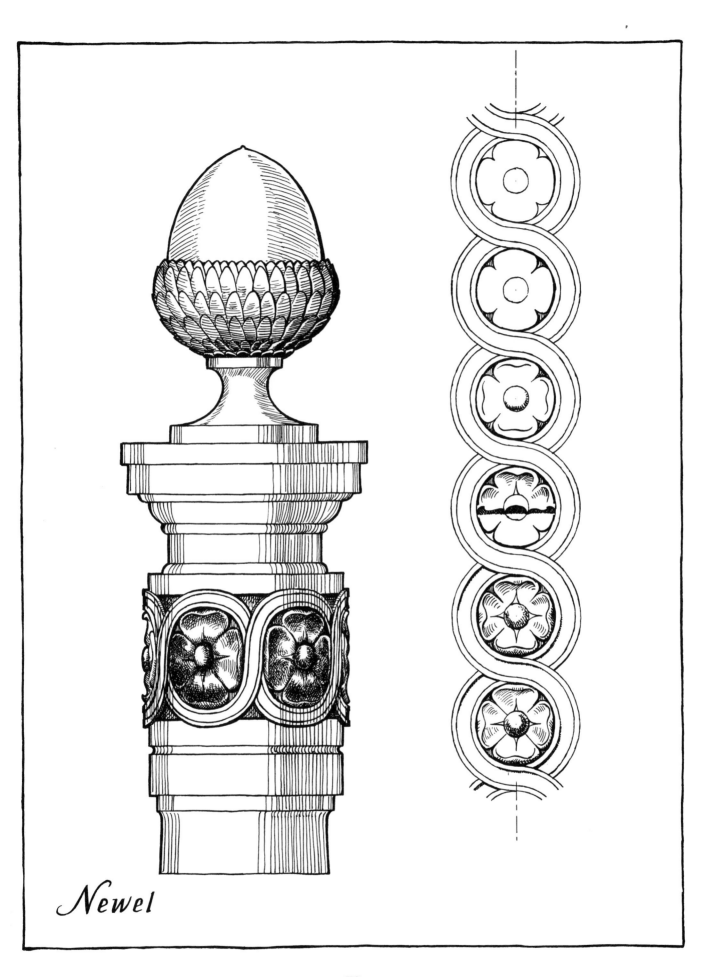

Newel

Bread Platters
Traditional designs

Early 1900's

Use dry, hard wood, about 1″ thick. The center of the board must be flat, and the border should slope slightly toward the outer rim, so as to minimize knife damage to the carving while in use.

The suggested border designs may be used on any of the shapes. Longer rectangular boards are also useful. If a board for carving meat is wanted, make a concave border channel to catch juices.

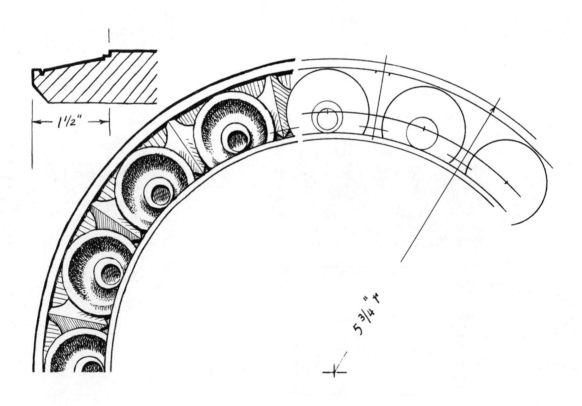

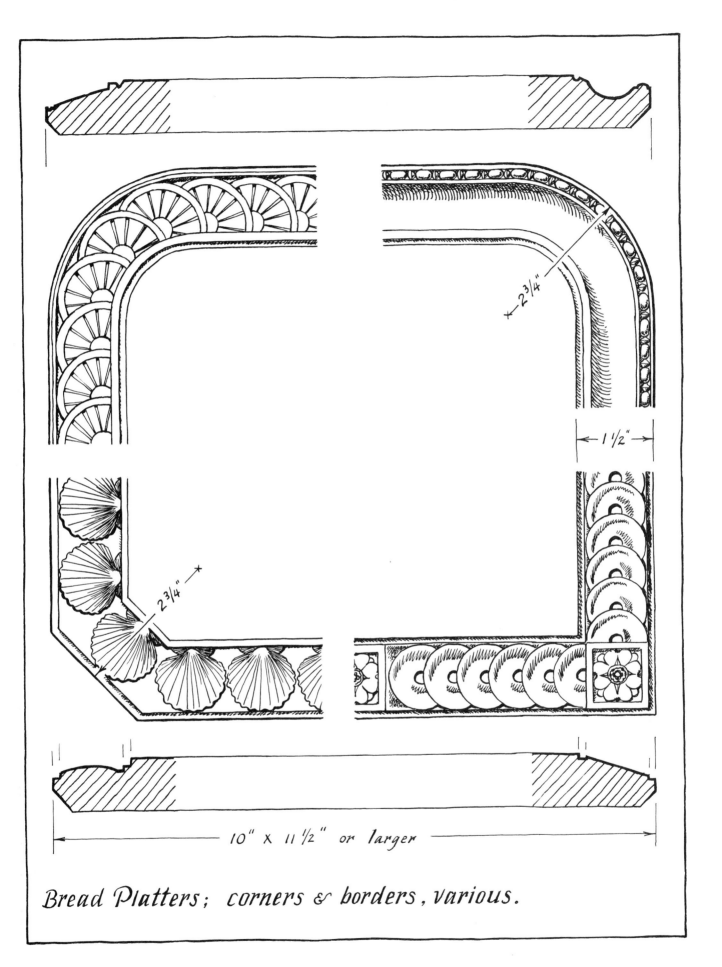

2³/₄"

1½"

2³/₄"

10" x 11½" or larger

Bread Platters; corners & borders, various.

81

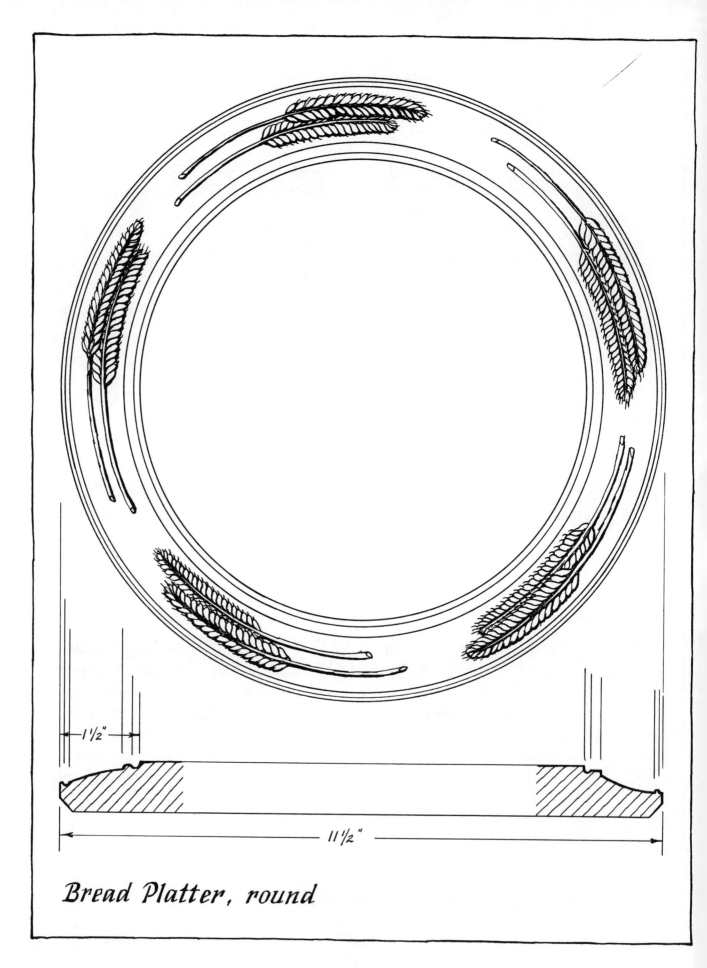

1½"

11½"

Bread Platter, round

SIGN DESIGN

The dedication in the opening portion of this book covers the work of an old world, well trained, professional carver who started in the early nineteen hundreds. Such training is no longer available. However, it is encouraging to note that splendid results in woodcarving can be achieved now-a-days by those who have no formal training at all. Witness the success of the Cohasset Woodcarvers. By determination, persistence, observation, and development of skills, a mathametics major and a physical education graduate have become the most sought-after carvers in eastern Massachusetts. Their ability to design, lay out, execute, and finish first class carvings has brought them work from all over the country. They attract commissions for carved signs, plaques, and three dimensional sculpture. Their shop includes equipment for cutting, glueing, painting and preservation, and gold leaf application. A professional approach, suitable work space, and proper equipment sets the scene, and when the product is superior the demand continues to grow.

Another example of a successful self-taught sign carver is Mr. Donald J. Neilly of lower Three Fathom Harbor, Nova Scotia, a retired Canadian Naval Pilot. Inspired by New England woodcarvers, he has established a name for himself by virtue of strict adherence to a very high self-imposed standard of quality.

PREPARATION OF SKETCHES

Prior to a full-size layout it is advisable to make "thumbnail" sketches. These quickly drawn idea-jottings may be of any convenient size, from calling card size up to post card size, or larger. Two or three or more will help crystalize your concept, and discussions of these with your client will help you reach agreement. Identify the business, or the farm, or the owner. Use symbols. Create images. Select significant details to enhance your design from things at hand, in books, from nature. For endings on quarter boards look at old silver spoon handles. Check out the details on a hundred dollar bill. Use flower and fruit motifs.

Eagle Sign

Composite Design   Contemporary

There are several options for this project. Carve a straightforward relief panel on plank stock, centering the entire design. Or, for a higher, more dramatic relief, make the eagle of 2″ or 3″ thick stock, glued up if necessary, and prepare the panel separately. The surface of the sign may be flat or convex. Suggested finish: the eagle, the egg and dart, and the lettering — gold leaf. The background of the sign could be dark stain.

For the egg and dart moulding maintain the approximate proportions shown here, regardless of the scale chosen for the job. With a compass make trial layouts for the motif. When it spaces out evenly draw two sections on card stock or other stiff paper. Cut a stencil of this and lay out the entire border, making the necessary adjustments before starting to carve.

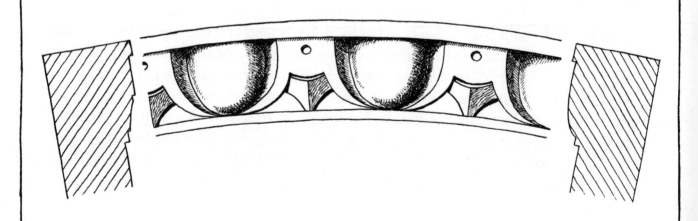

JOHN CURTIS

Eagle Sign

LAYOUT

There is no substitute for a careful, full-size working layout on paper, after agreement on conceptual sketches, and before one cuts into the wood. Resolve all details. The impact will be powerful when the design is simple, well arranged, and where possible, combining relief carving with the necessary lettering. The lettering should be as large as aesthetically possible, and the style and shape should be appropriate to the subject. Be very brief with words. Customers often want their entire history spelled out, but that does not make for a good sign, the principal requirement of which is that it be read at a glance. A few significant words will be the most effective.

After a satisfactory layout has been developed, transfer the drawing to the wood. At this stage adjustments still can be made, and strengthening and clarifying of lines can be finalized.

It is often useful to indicate by marking in red, or some other color, those areas which are highest, or areas to be left for carving at a later time.

PROPER SIZE

Many things will influence size. The local Building Inspector, or the Town Planning Board may have regulations to be observed. Also, certain purely mechanical and engineering considerations will have to be taken into account. Wind force, support structures, braces, retainers, weight, and material must be studied and resolved. To minimize racking, which in strong winds can destroy the sign, place suspension points on a hanging sign closer together than those on the element from which the sign is hung.

LETTERING

Lettering is usually the most important element of a sign. One's first glance signals an impression before one actually reads the words. Each carver must become a good self-critic. Particular attention must be given to producing sound work of a professional calibre following basic rules and traditions. Strive for smooth, flowing lines to form solid, graceful letters; these are not attainable by the use of purely mechanical methods alone. It is not easy to design correct forms, but with practice and diligent work on your layouts, you will find the appropriate relationship of shape, weight, and size of letters.

The use of commercial transfer letters, available at art or architectural supply stores, can be of some help. However, you will find that because of size, or style, or arrangement, or the customer's desires, you will eventually have to do it the hard way.

Spacing and arrangement of the words should be such as to avoid collisions between ascenders and descenders where lower case letters are involved. Beware also of stacking up more or less solid verticals when they coincide in a two or three line sign.

Negative spaces, that is, the spaces between the letters, not the space which each letter occupies, should look as if they were about equal in weight.

The weight of the uprights should be in good proportion to the height of each letter. When evaluating the impact of weight it is a good idea to consider the entire word, or the line as a whole.

Do whatever is necessary to prevent each letter from giving the appearance of not filling the space allotted to it. In particular watch out for:

O Q A N V W

Carved lettering should not look as if it had been done with a router. Preserve the handcarved effect. To accurately cut the "V" section-shape some carvers use a knife, usually made from an All Purpose knife with a short, specially ground 35° blade, because it is possible for them to attain greater accuracy with this tool than with chisels or gouges.

While they are perhaps not only the oldest shape for carved letter formation, the lights and reflections on "V"-cut letters seem to be the most pleasing.

Ornamentation can detract. When appropriate, flourishes or embellishments to letters should be confined to letters which lend themselves to ornamentation. Use it only on key capital letters, such as:

R N Q K G A M H

Lettering along curves can be accurately controlled by drawing parallel guide lines. Start with a center line representing the desired direction(s). With a pencil compass scribe a series of circles, representing the height of the lettering, using the centerline as your guide. Then join the edges of the circles with tangents.

Lettering on curved lines is always distorted, so be careful to observe rules about direction, weight, and both negative space and the space the letter occupies.

STYLE AND PROPORTION OF LETTERING

It is important to design signs which catch the eye, but it is prudent to keep the lettering fairly traditional and very readable. To this end one can work with a few tried and tested styles. For example:

the dignified   **ROMAN**

the versatile   **BLOCK**

the energetic   *ITALIC*

the flowing   *Script*

To produce handsome letters two important standards of proportion should be kept in mind:

- the thickness of the verticals. These should be about ⅛ or ⅙ of the height of the letter. However, the I is thicker, and those with thinner elements are:

N   M   W   A   V   X   Y   Z

- the approximate height to width ratio. This is illustrated below.

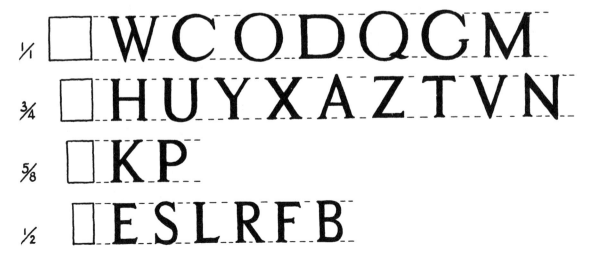

89

ROMAN

A B C D E F G H I J K L M N O P Q R
S T U V W X Y Z & 1 2 3 4 5 6 7 8 9 0

This alphabet, with its incised "v" shape, has serifs. These are horizontal cuts at the top and bottom of verticals. They are finishing touches, probably first developed by early Roman stone carvers because it is quicker and easier to do this than to finish off the end of a vertical by keeping it parallel and level with adjoining letters. In addition, letters with serifs appear more solid and readable. For wood carving this style is as natural and as easy as it is for marble.

BLOCK

A B C D E F G H I J K L M N O P Q R
S T U V W X Y Z & 1 2 3 4 5 6 7 8 9 0

Block letters have no serifs and all parts of the letters are of uniform thickness. The thickness, or weight, of the letters may vary with the layout requirements of the sign, or for some other consideration, such as for emphasis, or visual effect. Not an easy letter for carving, especially when raised. However, a shallow, incised block letter with gold or color added can be very effective.

For sign work the block letter thickness could be ⅛ or ⅙ of the height. In cross section the letter has parallel sides, and is flat if raised, and may be flat or half round if incised.

In cross section, whether raised or incised, the letter is flat; but make the sides slope to avoid the machine-made look.

A B C D E F G H I J K L M N O P Q R
S T U V W X Y Z & 1 2 3 4 5 6 7 8 9 0

The proportion of italic letters, developed from Roman capitals, takes a surprising change. Due to the apparent elongation, the narrow letters vary only slightly in width, while the wide letters must be made much narrower to look right. The judicious exercise of taste, and close attention to aesthetic values, are necessary to feel one's way along while laying out words in this alphabet. The verticals must be parallel as with other alphabets, but no letter can look as though it slants more than another. To this end lay out guide lines that slope. Then sketch in the letters and adjust until they look right.

It is suggested that you use italics for only a word or two, and that you confine them to eye level applications. More serious problems appear when perspective is involved, such as when the sign hangs high and one must stand close to read it.

Script

A B C D E F G H I J K L M
N O P Q R S T U V W X Y Z

a b c d e f g h i j k l m n o p q r
s t u v w x y z & 1 2 3 4 5 6 7 8 9 0

Script has a lightness, and is useful for special purposes, although it is not a carver's letter. It carries with it all of the problems of the italics. Its basic structure, spacing, and form must be correct. It can be eye-catching when used in exaggerated size, perhaps for a single word or two. Old French or Italian specimens are the best source material.

Is and looks like this

PLACEMENT

An important consideration is the placement of the sign. If it is to be seen and read from a distance, or if it is to hang rather low, the line of sight will be more nearly parallel to the ground, the effect will be as if the eye of the observer is more or less on line with the lettering. In this case the lettering should have normal form and proportion.

However, if the sign is to be hung high, and the observer is to see it from close by, then the line of sight will be very much more at an incline and the letters will look too short and fat.

To compensate for this illusionary effect, the letters should be somewhat elongated to make them look normal.

Is like this

but looks like this

Another thing to pay attention to is the direction in which the sign will face. The rays and heat of the sun have a significant effect. If it must face the afternoon sun take what measures you can to protect and preserve the wood and the surface. See page 95.

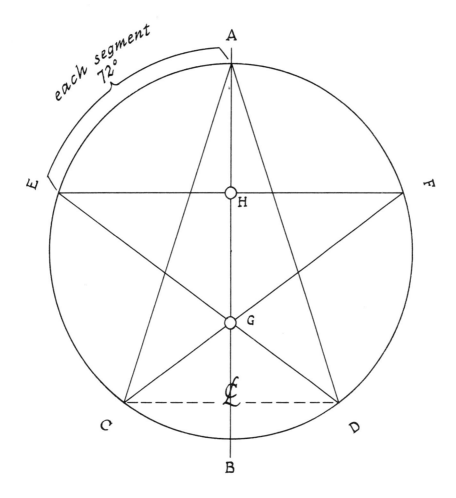

TO LAY OUT A STAR

For a perfect five-pointed star lay out a long vertical centerline. With the point of a compass on the middle of the center line scribe a circle with a radius equal to that of whatever protractor you may have. From point A (the intersection of the top of the circle and the centerline) lay off 72 degrees five times. Connect the points A-D, D-E, E-F, F-C, C-A.

TO MAKE A TEMPLATE

Using triangle A-D-C as a pattern cut a template of any handy material such as sheet brass, aluminum flashing, stencil board, or lucite. Exactly on the centerline make one or two locating holes; G, and for smaller stars at H, approximately.

TO USE THE TEMPLATE

Draw a circle of the size of the star desired. Erect the perpendicular centerline A-B. Place the apex point A of the template at the spot where the centerline intersects the top of the circle, and line up G or H on same centerline. Draw lines along both sides of the template to where they intersect the circle. Place template point on C, and then on D to draw the completing lines.

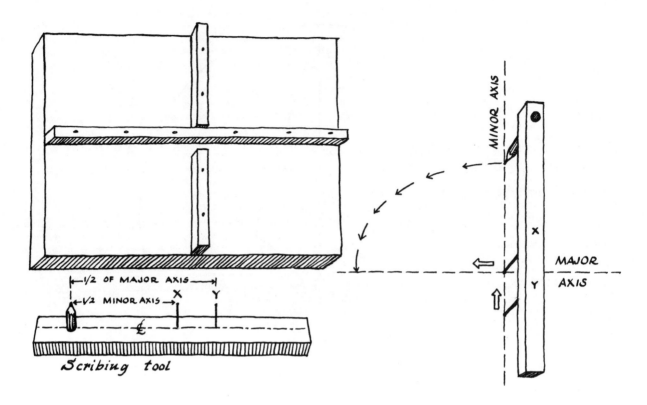

Figure 13

TO LAY OUT AN ELLIPSE

Directly on the wood draw a horizontal and a vertical axis. Measure off the proposed dimensions of the ellipse, for example major axis 24″ and minor axis 15″. Tack straight edges of wood along these two axes.

THE SCRIBING TOOL

Build a scribing tool; a length of wood 6″ or 8″ longer than ½ the major axis. It should be about 2″ wide and about 1″ thick. On the wide side draw a centerline. Near one end of this line drill a hole and insert a pencil, the point of which must lie on the centerline. At 7½″ (½ of the minor axis) from the point of the pencil drive a finishing nail, and another at 12″ (½ of the major axis). All three to be on the centerline and nearly the same height.

TO USE THE SCRIBING TOOL

With the pencil touching the wood at the top of the major axis (Figure 13), place X at the intersection of the two axes, and Y wherever it falls along the lower minor axis.

Concentrating on the nails, and holding them and the pencil squarely vertical, slide X to the left as Y moves up, thus rotating the pencil end through a quadrant of a perfect ellipse. Repetition of these maneuvers will produce the remaining quadrants.

MATERIALS

Wood should be dry and clear of knots and imperfections. Mahogany and bass wood are recommended. Green lumber and sappy pine, and woods that chip or split must never be used.

For outdoor use, a long soak in Watco Exterior wood finish oil is desirable because the wood ages naturally after this treatment. Maintenance is easy because rubbing more oil into the wood restores the finish.

If stain is to be used, the standard Cabot or Cuprinol types are stable and seem to work best.

Colonial oil paints such as Turco or Martin Senour are very appropriate, pleasing and durable. For coloring the details on special carvings of scenes or animals, etc. on signs high grade artist's tube oil paints are most satisfactory.

Gold leaf for exterior use must be 23 carat, while for interiors lesser fineness or even "composition" gold leaf, which contains some brass is acceptable. Striping around gold leaf is often done on outdoor work. It makes the lettering stand out and also seals the edges of the gold.

For the amateur, the use of Interlux, an exterior marine polyurethene may be an easy solution to finishing some signs, but interior polyurethene should never be used outdoors because it tends to peel and lift off paint or gold leaf.

For outdoor signs avoid lacquer. Waxes have a tendency to fade.

A finish produced by burning with a torch may have an interesting effect, but the oxidization speeds up the aging of the wood.

INDEX